Healthy Keto Vegetarian Diet

Lose Weight & Back in Shape with

Easy Tasty Recipes

Ricardo Abagnale

by reading this document, the reader agrees that under no circumstances is the author responsible for any losses, direct or indirect, which are incurred as a result of the use of information contained within this document, including, but not limited to, — errors, omissions, or inaccuracies.

Table of Contents

INTRODUCTION

The Ketogenic diet is truly life changing. The diet improves your overall health and helps you lose the extra weight in a matter of days. The diet will show its multiple benefits even from the beginning and it will become your new lifestyle really soon.

As soon as you embrace the Ketogenic diet, you will start to live a completely new life.

On the other hand, the vegetarian diet is such a healthy dietary option you can choose when trying to live healthy and also lose some weight.

The collection we bring to you today is actually a combination between the Ketogenic and vegetarian diets. You get to discover some amazing Ketogenic vegetarian dishes you can prepare in the comfort of your own home. All the dishes you found here follow both the Ketogenic and the vegetarian rules, they all taste delicious and rich and they are all easy to make.

We can assure you that such a combo is hard to find. So, start a keto diet with a vegetarian "touch" today. It will be both useful and fun!

So, what are you still waiting for? Get started with the Ketogenic diet and learn how to prepare the best and most flavored Ketogenic vegetarian dishes. Enjoy them all!

BREAKFAST

Coconut Waffles

Preparation time: 12 minutes

Cooking time: 5 minutes

Servings: 4

Nutritional Values (Per Serving):

- Calories: 247
- Fat: 19 g
- Carbohydrates: 6 g
- Sugar: 1 g
- Protein: 11 g
- Cholesterol: 309 mg

Ingredients:

- 1/3 cup coconut flour
- ½ teaspoon salt
- 4 tablespoons butter, melted
- 6 organic eggs
- 1/8 teaspoon Stevia drops
- ½ teaspoon baking powder

Directions:

1. Add eggs along with butter into your blender and blend until well combined.
2. Pour egg mixture into mixing bowl. Add coconut flour, Stevia, baking powder and salt, mix well. Set aside for 5 minutes.
3. Heat your waffle iron, once it is hot pour batter and cook for 5 minutes or according to your waffle iron instructions.
4. Serve and enjoy!

Coconut Pecan Porridge

Preparation time: 5 minutes

Cooking time: 5 minutes

Servings: 2

Nutritional Values (Per Serving):

- Calories: 489
- Fat: 47.9 g
- Carbohydrates: 15.1 g
- Sugar: 3.9 g
- Protein: 11.2 g
- Cholesterol: 0 mg

Ingredients:

- ½ teaspoon cinnamon
- ¼ cup pecans, chopped
- ¼ cup coconut, unsweetened, toasted 2 tablespoons chia seeds
- ¼ cup coconut milk
- ¾ cup almond milk, unsweetened
- ¼ cup almond butter
- 1 tablespoon coconut oil 2 tablespoons hemp seeds

Directions:

1. 1. Add almond butter, coconut oil, almond milk, coconut milk into a saucepan and simmer over medium heat for 5 minutes or so. Once your mixture has reached the point of becoming hot, remove it from heat.
2. Add toasted coconut, hemp seeds, chia seeds, cinnamon, and pecans, mix well. Set aside for 5 minutes.
3. Serve and enjoy!

Sage Rice and Veggies

Preparation time: 10 minutes

Cooking time: 12 minutes

Servings: 4

Nutritional Values (Per Serving):

- Calories 202
- Fat 17.1
- Fiber 6.3
- Carbs 13.2
- Protein 3.2

Ingredients:

- 2 cups cauliflower rice
- 2 tablespoons olive oil
- 1 avocado, peeled, pitted and cubed

- 1 green bell pepper, chopped
- 1 green chili, chopped
- 1 tomato, cubed
- 1 zucchini, cubed
- ½ cup radishes, halved
- 1 tablespoon sage, chopped
- 1 teaspoon lime juice
- A pinch of salt and black pepper

Directions:

1. Heat up a pan with the oil over medium heat, add the green chili and the cauliflower rice and sauté for 2 minutes.
2. Add the avocado, bell pepper and the other ingredients, toss, cook over medium heat for 10 minutes more, divide between plates and serve.

Cauliflower Rice and Chia Mix

Preparation time: 10 minutes

Cooking time: 15 minutes

Servings: 4

Nutritional Values (Per Serving):

- calories 220
- fat 19.6
- fiber 6.9
- carbs 10.4
- protein 4.1

Ingredients:

- 2 cups cauliflower rice
- 2 tablespoons chia seeds
- ½ cup radishes, halved
- ½ cup chives, chopped
- 2 tablespoons avocado oil

- Zest of 1 lime, grated
- 1 cup coconut cream

Directions:

1. Heat up a pan with the oil over medium heat, add the cauliflower rice, chia seeds and the other ingredients, toss, cook for 15 minutes, divide into bowls and serve.

Fruity Cauliflower Rice Bowls

Preparation time: 10 minutes

Cooking time: 0 minutes

Servings: 4

Nutritional Values (Per Serving):

- calories 138
- fat 10.9
- fiber 5.3
- carbs 11.1
- protein 1.8

Ingredients:

- ½ cup blackberries, halved
- ½ cup grapes, halved
- 2 cups cauliflower rice, steamed
- 1 cup cherry tomatoes, halved
- 1 avocado, peeled, pitted and cubed

- 2 tablespoons avocado oil
- Juice of 1 lime

Directions:

1. In a salad bowl, combine the cauliflower rice with the berries and the other ingredients, toss, divide into smaller bowls and serve.

Watercress Bowls

Preparation time: 10 minutes

Cooking time: 0 minutes

Servings: 4

Nutritional Values (Per Serving):

- Calories 28
- Fat 1.8
- Fiber 1
- Carbs 2.7
- Protein 1

Ingredients:

- 1 cup watercress
- ¼ cup grapes, halved
- ½ cup cherry tomatoes, halved
- 1 tablespoon almonds, chopped
- 1 tablespoon chives, chopped

- ¼ cup baby spinach
- 2 tablespoons avocado oil
- 2 tablespoons lime juice

Directions:

1. In a bowl, combine the watercress with the grapes and the other ingredients, toss well, divide into smaller bowls and serve.

Arugula Tomato Salad

Preparation time: 20 minutes

Servings: 2

Nutritional Values (Per Serving):

- Calories: 262
- Fat: 26.7 g
- Carbohydrates: 6 g
- Sugar: 3.1 g
- Protein: 2.1 g
- Cholesterol: 0 mg

Ingredients:

- 4 tablespoons olive oil
- 1 cup cherry tomatoes, halved
- 3 cups arugula, washed, drained
- 1 small red onion, chopped
- 4 tablespoons capers, canned, drained
- 2 tablespoons basil, fresh, chopped

Directions:

1. Add all ingredients into mixing bowl and toss. Serve fresh and enjoy!

Spicy Asian Broccoli

Preparation time: 25 minutes

Cooking time: 8 minutes

Servings: 4

Nutritional Values (Per Servings):

- Calories: 294
- Fat: 26.6 g
- Carbohydrates: 9.4 g
- Sugar: 3.2 g
- Protein: 6.3 g
- Cholesterol: 0 mg

Ingredients:

- 2 fresh limes' juice
- 2 small broccoli, cut into florets
- 2 teaspoon chili pepper, chopped
- 2 tablespoons ginger, fresh, grated

- 4 garlic cloves, chopped
- 8 tablespoons olive oil

Directions:

1. Add your broccoli florets into your steamer and steam them for 8 minutes. Meanwhile, to prepare dressing, add lime juice, garlic, chili pepper, oil, and ginger in a small mixing bowl and combine. Add steamed broccoli in a large mixing bowl and drizzle over it the dressing. Toss to blend. Serve and enjoy!

Tomato Cucumber Cheese Salad

Preparation time: 15 minutes

Servings: 2

Nutritional Values (Per Serving):

- Calories: 609
- Fat: 50.5 g
- Carbohydrates: 13.7 g
- Sugar: 7.5 g
- Protein: 27.2 g
- Cholesterol: 47 mg

Ingredients:

- 2 cups tomatoes, sliced
- 2 cucumbers, peeled, sliced
- 2 spring onions, sliced
- 7-ounces mozzarella cheese, chopped
- 12 black olives

- 2 teaspoons basil pesto
- 2 tablespoons extra-virgin olive oil
- 2 tablespoons basil, fresh, chopped

Directions:

1. In a large salad bowl, add basil pesto and cheese. Mix well. Add remaining ingredients into a bowl and toss to blend. Serve fresh and enjoy!

Healthy Brussels Sprout Salad

Preparation time: 15 minutes

Servings: 1

Nutritional Values (Per Serving):

- Calories: 156
- Fat: 9.6 g
- Carbohydrates: 10.7 g
- Sugar: 2.5 g
- Cholesterol: 10 mg
- Protein: 10

Ingredients:

- ½ teaspoon apple cider vinegar
- 6 Brussels sprouts, washed, sliced
- 1 tablespoon Parmesan cheese, fresh, grated
- 1 teaspoon extra-virgin olive oil
- ¼ teaspoon pepper

- ¼ teaspoon sea salt

Directions:

1. Add all your ingredients into a large salad bowl, toss to blend. Serve and enjoy!

Radish Hash Browns

Preparation time: 10 minutes

Cooking time: 10 minutes

Servings: 4

Nutritional Values (Per Serving):

- Calories: 176
- Fat: 10.4 g
- Carbohydrates: 13 g
- Sugar: 4 g
- Cholesterol: 116 mg
- Protein: 7.9 g

Ingredients:

- 2 shallots, peeled, sliced
- ¼ teaspoon thyme
- ¼ teaspoon paprika
- 1 organic egg
- 1 tablespoon coconut flour

- 2 ounces cheddar cheese
- 1 lb. radishes, shredded
- ¼ teaspoon pepper
- ¼ teaspoon sea salt

Directions:

1. Add ingredients into a mixing bowl, except for the butter and mix well.
2. Melt the butter in a pan over medium heat.
3. Add a scoop of mixture into the pan and fry until lightly browned on both sides.
4. Serve and enjoy!

Baked Broccoli and Pine Nuts

Preparation time: 10 minutes

Cooking time: 30 minutes

Servings: 4

Nutritional Values (Per Serving):

- Calories 220
- Fat 6
- Fiber 2
- Carbs 7
- Protein 6

Ingredients:

- 2 tablespoons olive oil
- 1 pound broccoli florets
- 1 tablespoon garlic, minced

- 1 tablespoon pine nuts, toasted
- 1 tablespoon lemon juice
- 2 teaspoons mustard
- A pinch of salt and black pepper

Directions:

1. In a roasting pan, combine the broccoli with the oil, the garlic and the other ingredients, toss and bake at 380 degrees F for 30 minutes.
2. Divide everything between plates and serve as a side dish.

Quinoa and Peas

Preparation time: 10 minutes

Cooking time: 30 minutes

Servings: 4

Nutritional Values (Per Serving):

- Calories 202
- Fat 3
- Fiber 3
- Carbs 11
- Protein 6

Ingredients:

- 1 yellow onion, chopped
- 1 tomato, cubed
- 1 cup quinoa
- 3 cups vegetable stock
- 1 tablespoon olive oil

- 1 cup peas
- 1 tablespoon cilantro, chopped
- A pinch of salt and black pepper

Directions:

1. Heat up a pot with the oil over medium heat, add the onion, stir and sauté for 5 minutes.
2. Add the quinoa, the stock and the other ingredients, toss, bring to a simmer and cook over medium heat for 25 minutes.
3. Divide everything between plates and serve as a side dish.

Basil Green Beans

Preparation time: 10 minutes

Cooking time: 20 minutes

Servings: 4

Nutritional Values (Per Serving):

- Calories 221
- Fat 5
- Fiber 8
- Carbs 10
- Protein 8

Ingredients:

- 1 yellow onion, chopped
- 1 pound green beans, trimmed and halved
- 1 tablespoon avocado oil
- 2 teaspoons basil, dried

- A pinch of salt and black pepper
- 1 tablespoon tomato sauce

Directions:

1. Heat up a pan with the oil over medium-high heat, add the onion and sauté for 5 minutes.
2. Add the green beans and the other ingredients, toss, cook for 15 minutes more.
3. Divide everything between plates and serve as a side dish.

Balsamic Brussels Sprouts

Preparation time: 10 minutes

Cooking time: 20 minutes

Servings: 4

Nutritional Values (Per Serving):

- Calories 108
- Fat 1.2
- Fiber 8.7
- Carbs 21.7
- Protein 7.9

Ingredients:

- 2 pounds Brussels sprouts, trimmed and halved
- 1 tablespoon avocado oil
- 2 tablespoons balsamic vinegar
- 3 garlic cloves, minced
- 1 tablespoon cilantro, chopped
- A pinch of salt and black pepper

Directions:

1. Heat up a pan with the oil over medium-high heat, add the garlic and sauté for 2 minutes.
2. Add the sprouts and the other ingredients, toss, cook over medium heat for 18 minutes more, divide between plates and serve.

Beet and Cabbage

Preparation time: 10 minutes

Cooking time: 20 minutes

Servings: 4

Nutritional Values (Per Serving):

- Calories 128
- Fat 7.3
- Fiber 5.6
- Carbs 15.6
- Protein 3.1

Ingredients:

- 1 green cabbage head, shredded
- 1 yellow onion, chopped
- 1 beet, peeled and cubed
- ½ cup chicken stock
- 2 tablespoons olive oil

- A pinch of salt and black pepper
- 2 tablespoons chives, chopped

Directions:

1. Heat up a pan with the oil over medium heat, add the onion and sauté for 5 minutes.
2. Add the cabbage and the other ingredients, toss, cook over medium heat for 15 minutes more, divide between plates and serve.

Chili Asparagus

Preparation time: 10 minutes

Cooking time: 15 minutes

Servings: 4

Nutritional Values (Per Serving):

- Calories 80
- Fat 7.2
- Fiber 1.4
- Carbs 4.4
- Protein 1

Ingredients:

- 1 yellow onion, chopped
- 2 tablespoons olive oil
- 1 bunch asparagus, trimmed and halved
- 2 garlic cloves, minced

- 1 teaspoon chili powder
- ¼ cup cilantro, chopped

Directions:

1. Heat up a pan with the oil over medium-high heat, add the onion and the garlic and sauté for 5 minutes.
2. Add the asparagus and the other ingredients, toss, cook for 10 minutes, divide between plates and serve.

Artichokes with Horseradish Sauce

Preparation time: 10 minutes

Cooking time: 45 minutes

Servings: 2

Nutritional Values (Per Serving):

- Calories 107
- Fat 5, Fiber 3,3
- Carbs 14,9
- Protein 1,7

Ingredients:

- 1 tablespoon horseradish, prepared
- 2 tablespoons mayonnaise

- A pinch of sea salt
- Black pepper to taste
- 1 teaspoon lemon juice
- 3 cups artichoke hearts
- 1 tablespoon lemon juice

Directions:

1. In a bowl, mix horseradish with mayo, a pinch of sea salt, black pepper and 1 teaspoon lemon juice, whisk well and leave aside for now.
2. Arrange artichoke hearts on a lined baking sheet, drizzle 2 tablespoons olive oil over them, 1 tablespoon lemon juice and sprinkle a pinch of salt and some black pepper.
3. Toss to coat well, place in the oven at 425 degrees F and roast for 45 minutes.
4. Divide artichoke hearts between plates and serve with the horseradish sauce on top.
5. Enjoy!

Grilled Artichokes

Preparation time: 10 minutes

Cooking time: 25 minutes

Servings: 4

Nutritional Values (Per Serving):

- calories 98
- fat 7,1
- fiber 4,4
- carbs 8,5
- protein 2,7

Ingredients:

- 2 artichokes, trimmed and halved
- Juice of 1 lemon
- 1 tablespoons lemon zest grated
- 1 rosemary spring, chopped
- 2 tablespoons olive oil
- A pinch of sea salt
- Black pepper to taste

Directions:

1. Put water in a large saucepan, add a pinch of salt and lemon juice, bring to a boil over medium-high heat, add artichokes, boil for 15 minutes, drain and leave them to cool down.
2. Drizzle olive oil over them, season with black pepper to taste, sprinkle lemon zest and rosemary, stir well and place them under a preheated grill.
3. Broil artichokes over medium-high heat for 5 minutes on each side, divide them between plates and serve.
4. Enjoy!

Artichokes and Tomatoes Dip

Preparation time: 10 minutes

Cooking time: 30 minutes

Servings: 4

Nutritional Values (Per Serving):

- Calories 193
- Fat 14,5
- Fiber 6,1
- Carbs 16,9
- Protein 4,1

Ingredients:

- 2 artichokes, cut in halves and trimmed
- Juice from 3 lemons
- 4 sun-dried tomatoes, chopped
- A bunch of parsley, chopped
- A bunch of basil, chopped

- 1 garlic clove, minced
- 4 tablespoons olive oil
- Black pepper to taste

Directions:

1. In a bowl, mix artichokes with lemon juice from 1 lemon, some black pepper and toss to coat.
2. Transfer to a large saucepan, add water to cover, bring to a boil over medium-high heat, cook for 30 minutes and drain.
3. In a food processor, mix the rest of the lemon juice with tomatoes, parsley, basil, garlic, black pepper and olive oil and blend well.
4. Divide artichokes between plates and top each with the tomatoes dip.
5. Enjoy!

Carrots and Lime Mix

Preparation time: 10 minutes

Cooking time: 30 minutes

Servings: 6

Nutritional Values (Per Serving):

- Calories 95
- Fat 6,6
- Fiber 2,9
- Carbs 9,1
- Protein 0,9

Ingredients:

- 1 and ¼ pounds baby carrots
- 3 tablespoons ghee, melted
- 8 garlic cloves, minced
- A pinch of sea salt
- Black pepper to taste

- Zest of 2 limes, grated
- ½ teaspoon chili powder

Directions:

1. In a bowl, mix baby carrots with ghee, garlic, a pinch of salt, black pepper to taste, chili powder and stir well.
2. Spread carrots on a lined baking sheet, place in the oven at 400 degrees F and roast for 15 minutes.
3. Take carrots out of the oven, shake baking sheet, place in the oven again and roast for 15 minutes more.
4. Divide between plates and serve with lime on top.
5. Enjoy!

Maple Glazed Carrots

Preparation time: 10 minutes

Cooking time: 15 minutes

Servings: 4

Nutritional Values (Per Serving):

- Calories 130
- Fat 6,8
- Fiber 3
- Carbs 17,4
- Protein 1,1

Ingredients:

- 1 pound carrots, sliced
- 1 tablespoon coconut oil
- 1 tablespoon ghee
- ½ cup pineapple juice
- 1 teaspoon ginger, grated

- ½ tablespoon maple syrup
- ½ teaspoon nutmeg
- 1 tablespoon parsley, chopped

Directions:

1. Heat a pan with the ghee and the oil over medium-high heat, add ginger, stir and cook for 2 minutes.
2. Add carrots, stir and cook for 5 minutes.
3. Add pineapple juice, maple syrup and nutmeg, stir and cook for 5 minutes more.
4. Add parsley, stir, cook for 3 minutes, divide between plates and serve.
5. Enjoy!

Lemony Lentil and Rice Soup

Preparation time: 15 minutes

Cooking time: 1hour 10 minutes

Servings: 6

Ingredients:

- 2 tablespoons olive oil
- 1 medium onion, chopped
- 1 medium carrot, cut into 1⁄4-inch dice
- 1 celery rib, cut into 1⁄4-inch dice
- 11⁄4 cups brown lentils, picked over, rinsed, and drained
- 3⁄4 cup long-grain brown rice
- 1 14.5-ouncecan crushed tomatoes
- 2 cups tomato juice
- 2 bay leaves
- 1⁄2 teaspoon ground cumin
- 6 cups water

- 1 teaspoon salt
- 1⁄4 teaspoon freshly ground black pepper
- 1 tablespoon fresh lemon juice
- 2 tablespoons minced fresh parsley

Directions:

1. In a large soup pot, heat the oil over medium heat. Add the onion, carrot, and celery. Cover and cook until tender, about 10 minutes.
2. Add the lentils, rice, tomatoes, tomato juice, bay leaves, cumin, water, salt, and pepper. Bring to a boil, then reduce heat to medium low, and simmer, uncovered, until lentils and rice are tender, about 1 hour.
3. Just before serving, remove and discard the bay leaves, and stir in the lemon juice and parsley. Taste, adjusting seasonings if necessary, and serve.

Balsamic Lentil Stew

Preparation time: 10 minutes

Cooking time: 30 minutes

Servings: 5

Nutrition (2 cups)

- Calories: 353
- Protein: 22g
- Total fat: 2g
- Saturated fat: 0g
- Carbohydrates: 67g
- Fiber: 27g

Ingredients:

- 1 teaspoon olive oil
- 4 carrots, peeled and chopped
- 1 onion, chopped
- 3 garlic cloves, minced

- 2 tablespoons balsamic vinegar
- 4 cups Economical Vegetable Broth or water
- 1 28-ouncecan crushed tomatoes
- 1 tablespoon sugar
- 2 cups dried lentils or 2 15-ouncecans lentils, drained and rinsed
- 1 teaspoon salt
- Freshly ground black pepper

Directions:

1. Preparing the ingredients
2. Heat the olive oil in a large soup pot over medium heat.
3. Add the carrots, onion, and garlic and sauté for about 5 minutes, until the vegetables are softened. Pour in the vinegar, and let it sizzle to deglaze the bottom of the pot. Add the vegetable broth, tomatoes, sugar, and lentils.
4. Bring to a boil, then reduce the heat to low. Simmer for about 25 minutes, until the lentils are soft. Add the salt and season to taste with pepper. Leftovers will keep in an airtight container for up to 1 week in the refrigerator or up to 1 month in the freezer.

Tomato Orzo Soup

Preparation time: 5 minutes

Cooking time: 30 minutes

Servings: 4

Ingredients:

- 1 tablespoon olive oil
- 1 medium onion, chopped
- 1 celery rib, minced
- 3 garlic cloves, minced
- 1 28-ouncecan crushed tomatoes
- 3 cups chopped fresh ripe tomatoes
- 2 tablespoons tomato paste
- 3 cups vegetable broth (homemade, store-bought or water)

- 2 bay leaves
- Salt and freshly ground black pepper
- 1 cup plain unsweetened soy milk
- 1½ cups cooked orzo
- 2 tablespoons chopped fresh basil, for garnish

Directions:

1. In large soup pot, heat the oil over medium heat. Add the onion, celery, and garlic. Cover and cook until softened, about 5 minutes. Stir in the canned and fresh tomatoes, tomato paste, broth, sugar, and bay leaves. Season with salt and pepper to taste and bring to a boil. Reduce the heat to low, cover, and simmer, uncovered, until the vegetables are tender, about 20 minutes.

2. Remove and discard bay leaves. Puree the soup in the pot with an immersion blender or in a blender or food processor, in batches if necessary, and return to the pot. Stir in the soy milk, taste, adjusting seasonings if necessary, and heat through.

3. Spoon about ⅓ cup of the orzo into the bottom of each bowl, ladle the hot soup on top, and serve sprinkled with the basil.

Creamy Mushrooms with Shirataki

Preparation time: 25 minutes

Serving: 4

Nutritional Values (Per Serving):

- Calories:673
- Total Fat:58.8g
- Saturated Fat:36.3g
- Total Carbs: 16g
- Dietary Fiber:7
- Sugar:2 g
- Protein: 26g
- Sodium:760 mg

Ingredients:

For the angel hair shirataki:

- 2 (8 oz) packs angel hair shirataki

For the creamy mushrooms:

- 4 tbsp olive oil
- 1 lb sliced cremini mushrooms
- 3 shallots, finely chopped
- 6 garlic cloves, minced
- 2 tsp red chili flakes
- ¼ cup white wine
- ½ cup vegetable stock
- 1 ½ cups coconut cream
- 2 tbsp chopped fresh parsley
- Salt and black pepper to taste

Directions:

For the angel hair shirataki:

1. Bring 2 cups of water to a boil in a medium pot over medium heat.

2. Strain the shirataki pasta through a colander and rinse very well under hot running water.
3. Drain properly and transfer the shirataki pasta into the boiling water. Cook for 3 minutes and strain again.
4. Place a large dry skillet over medium heat and stir-fry the shirataki pasta until visibly dry, 1 to 2 minutes. Take off the heat and set aside.

For the creamy mushrooms:

5. Heat the olive oil in a large skillet and sauté the mushrooms, shallots, garlic, and chili flakes until softened and fragrant, 3 minutes.
6. Mix in the white wine and vegetable stock. Allow boiling and whisk in the remaining butter and then the coconut cream.
7. Taste the sauce and adjust the taste with salt, black pepper, and mix in the parsley.
8. Pour in the shirataki pasta, mussels and toss well in the sauce.
9. Serve afterwards.

Squash Spaghetti

Preparation time: 1 hour and 20 minutes

Serving: 4

Nutritional Values (Per Serving):

- Calories:865
- Total Fat:80.2g
- Saturated Fat:56.8g
- Total Carbs: 19g
- Dietary Fiber:5g
- Sugar: 5g
- Protein: 28g
- Sodium: 1775mg

Ingredients:

For the pasta:

- 2 medium spaghetti squashes, halved
- 2 tbsp olive oil

For the sauce:

- 2 tbsp butter
- 1 lb tempeh, crumbled
- ½ tsp garlic powder
- Salt and black pepper to taste
- 1 tsp arrowroot starch
- 1 ½ cups coconut cream
- A pinch of nutmeg
- 1/3 cup finely grated parmesan cheese
- 1/3 cup finely grated tempeh mozzarella cheese

Directions:

1. Preheat the oven to 375 F and line a baking dish with foil. Set aside.
2. Season the squash with the olive oil, salt, and black pepper. Place the squash on the baking dish, open side up and roast for 45 to 50 minutes until the squash is tender.
3. When ready, remove the squash from the oven, allow cooling and use two forks to shred the inner part of the noodles. Set aside.

4. Melt the butter in a medium pot, add the tempeh, garlic powder, salt, and black pepper, cook until brown, 10 minutes.
5. Stir in the arrowroot starch, coconut cream, and nutmeg. Cook until the sauce thickens, 2 to 3 minutes.
6. Spoon the sauce into the squashes and cover with the parmesan and mozzarella cheeses.
7. Place under the oven's broiler and cook until the cheeses melt and golden brown, 2 to 3 minutes.
8. Remove from the oven and serve warm.

Giardiniera

Preparation time: 15 minutes

Cooking time: 0 minutes

Servings: 6

Ingredients:

- 1 medium carrot, cut into 1/4-inch rounds
- 1 medium red bell pepper, cut into 1/2-inch dice
- 1 cup small cauliflower florets
- 2 celery ribs, finely chopped
- 1/2 cup chopped onion
- 2 tablespoons salt (optional)
- 1/4 cup sliced pimiento-stuffed green olives
- 1 garlic clove, minced
- 1/2 teaspoon sugar (optional)
- 1/2 teaspoon crushed red pepper
- 1/4 teaspoon freshly ground black pepper

- 3 tablespoons white wine vinegar
- 1/3 cup olive oil

Directions:

1. In a large bowl, combine the carrot, bell pepper, cauliflower, celery, and onion. Stir in the salt and add enough cold water to cover. Tightly cover the bowl and refrigerate for 4 to 6 hours.

2. Drain and rinse the vegetables and place them in a large bowl. Add the olives and set aside.

3. In a small bowl, combine the garlic, sugar, crushed red pepper, black pepper, vinegar, and oil, and mix well. Pour the dressing over the vegetables and toss gently to combine. Cover and refrigerate overnight before serving.

Creamy Avocado-Dressed Kale Salad

Preparation time: 10 minutes

Cooking time: 20 minutes

Servings: 4

Nutrition:

- Calories: 225
- Total fat: 7g
- Carbs: 37g
- Fiber: 7g
- Protein: 7g

Ingredients:

For The Dressing

- 1 avocado, peeled and pitted

- 1 tablespoon fresh lemon juice, or 1 teaspoon lemon juice concentrate and 2 teaspoons water
- 1 tablespoon fresh or dried dill
- 1 small garlic clove, pressed
- 1 scallion, chopped
- Pinch sea salt
- ¼ cup water

For The Salad

- 8 large kale leaves
- ½ cup chopped green beans, raw or lightly steamed
- 1 cup cherry tomatoes, halved
- 1 bell pepper, chopped
- 2 scallions, chopped
- 2 cups cooked millet, or other cooked whole grain, such as quinoa or brown rice Hummus (optional)

Directions:

For the Dressing:

1. Put all the ingredients in a blender or food processor. Purée until smooth, then add water as necessary to get

the consistency you're looking for in your dressing. Taste for seasoning, and add more salt if you need to.

For the Salad:

2. Chop the kale, removing the stems if you want your salad less bitter, and then massage the leaves with your fingers until it wilts and gets a bit moist, about 2 minutes. You can use a pinch salt if you like to help it soften. Toss the kale with the green beans, cherry tomatoes, bell pepper, scallions, millet, and the dressing. Pile the salad onto plates, and top them off with a spoonful of hummus (if using).

Indonesian-Style Potato Salad

Preparation time: 10 minutes

Cooking time: 30 minutes

Servings: 4 to 6

Ingredients:

- 1½ pounds small white potatoes, unpeeled
- 1 cup frozen peas, thawed
- ½ cup shredded carrot
- 4 green onions, chopped
- 1 tablespoon grapeseed oil
- 1 garlic clove, minced
- ⅓ cup creamy peanut butter

- ½ teaspoon Asian chili paste
- 2 tablespoons soy sauce
- 1 tablespoon rice vinegar
- ¾ cup unsweetened coconut milk
- 3 tablespoons chopped unsalted roasted peanuts, for garnish

Directions:

1. In a large pot of boiling salted water, cook the potatoes until tender, 20 to 30 minutes. Drain well and set aside to cool.
2. When cool enough to handle, cut the potatoes into 1-inch chunks and transfer to a large bowl. Add the peas, carrot, and green onions, and set aside.
3. In a small saucepan, heat the oil over medium heat. Add the garlic and cook until fragrant, about 30 seconds. Stir in the peanut butter, chili paste, soy sauce, vinegar, and about half of the coconut milk. Simmer over medium heat for 5 minutes, stirring frequently to make a smooth sauce. Add as much of the remaining coconut milk as needed for a creamy consistency. Pour the dressing over the salad and toss well to combine. Garnish with peanuts and serve.

Roasted Beet and Avocado Salad

Preparation time: 10 minutes

Cooking time: 30minutes

Servings: 2

Nutrition:

- Calories: 167
- Total fat: 13g
- Carbs: 15g
- Fiber: 5g
- Protein: 4g

Ingredients:

- 2 beets, peeled and thinly sliced
- 1 teaspoon olive oil
- Pinch sea salt
- 1 avocado
- 2 cups mixed greens

- 3 to 4 tablespoons Creamy Balsamic Dressing
- 2 tablespoons chopped almonds, pumpkin seeds, or sunflower seeds (raw or toasted)

Directions:

1. Preheat the oven to 400°F.
2. Put the beets, oil, and salt in a large bowl, and toss the beets with your hands to coat. Lay them in a single layer in a large baking dish, and roast them in the oven 20 to 30 minutes, or until they're softened and slightly browned around the edges.
3. While the beets are roasting, cut the avocado in half and take the pit out. Scoop the flesh out, as intact as possible, and slice it into crescents.
4. Once the beets are cooked, lay slices out on two plates and top each beet slice with a similar-size avocado slice.
5. Top with a handful of mixed greens. Drizzle the dressing over everything, and sprinkle on a few chopped almonds.

Arugula Dip

Preparation time: 10 minutes

Cooking time: 0 minutes

Servings: 4

Nutritional Values (Per Serving):

- Calories 100
- Fat 0
- Fiber 1
- Carbs 1
- Protein 3

Ingredients:

- ½ cup coconut cream
- 2 cups baby arugula
- Juice of 1 lime

- 2 tablespoons walnuts, chopped
- 2 tablespoons olive oil
- A pinch of salt and black pepper
- 2 garlic cloves minced
- ¼ teaspoon red pepper flakes, crushed

Directions:

In a blender, combine the arugula with the cream, lime juice and the otheringredients, pulse well, divide into bowls and serve as a party dip.

Coconut Bites

Preparation time: 10 minutes

Cooking time: 25 minutes

Servings: 6

Nutritional Values (Per Serving):

- calories 112
- fat 3
- fiber 3
- carbs 3
- protein 8

Ingredients:

- 1 cup coconut milk
- 1 and ½ cup coconut flesh, unsweetened and shredded A pinch of salt
- ¼ cup chives, chopped
- 2 teaspoons rosemary, dried

- Cooking spray

Directions:

1. In a pan, combine the coconut with the coconut milk and the otheringredients except the cooking sp ray, whisk and cook over medium heat for 10 minutes.
2. Take spoonfuls of this mix, shape medium balls, arrange them all on a baking sheet lined with parchment paper, grease them with the cooking spray, and cook at 450 degrees F for 15 minutes.
3. Serve the coconut bites cold.

Basil Eggplant Tapenade

Preparation time: 10 minutes

Cooking time: 15 minutes

Servings: 4

Nutritional Values (Per Serving):

- calories 121
- fat 3
- fiber 1
- carbs 8
- protein 12

Ingredients:

- 1 cup cherry tomatoes, cubed
- 2 eggplants, cubed
- 2 tablespoons kalamata olives, pitted and cubed
- 1 avocado, peeled, pitted and cubed
- 2 tablespoons olive oil

- 3 garlic cloves, minced
- 2 teaspoons balsamic vinegar
- 1 tablespoon basil, chopped
- A pinch of salt and black pepper

Directions:

1. Heat up a pan with the oil over medium heat, add the garlic, salt and pepper and sauté for 2 minutes.
2. Add the tomatoes, eggplants and the otheringredients, toss, cook over medium heat for 13 minutes, divide into small bowls and serve as an appetizer.

Hot Eggplant and Broccoli Spread

Preparation time: 10 minutes

Cooking time: 25 minutes

Servings: 8

Nutritional Values (Per Serving):

- calories 192
- fat 5
- fiber 7
- carbs 9
- protein 8

Ingredients:

- ½ cup walnuts, chopped
- 2 eggplants, cubed
- 1 cup broccoli florets

- 1 cup coconut cream
- 1 teaspoon hot paprika
- ½ teaspoon chili powder
- A pinch of salt and black pepper
- ½ teaspoon garlic powder
- 1 teaspoon cumin, ground
- ½ teaspoon rosemary, dried

Directions:

1. Heat up a pan with the cream over medium heat, add the walnuts, eggplants, broccoli and the otheringredients, stir, cook for 25 minutes and transfer to a blender.
2. Pulse well, divide into bowls and serve as a party spread.

Almond and Pine Nuts Spread

Preparation time: 10 minutes

Cooking time: 15 minutes

Servings: 8

Nutritional Values (Per Serving):

- Calories 112
- Fat 5
- Fiber 2
- Carbs 8
- Protein 10

Ingredients:

- 1 cup coconut cream
- ½ cup almonds, chopped
- 2 tablespoons pine nuts, toasted
- 1 tablespoon olive oil
- 1 teaspoon sage, ground
- 1 teaspoon chili powder
- A pinch of salt and black pepper

Directions:

1. In a pot, combine the almonds with the pine nuts, cream and the otheringredients, stir, cook over medium heat for 15 minutes and transfer to a blender.
2. Pulse well, divide into bowls and serve as a party spread.

Fat Free Apple Cake

Preparation time: 20 Minutes

Servings: 8

Ingredients:

- 2 granny smith apples, peeled, cored, and diced
- 1¾ cups unbleached all-purpose flour
- ⅔ cup packed light brown sugar
- ½ cup applesauce
- 1 tablespoon freshly squeezed lemon juice
- 1½ teaspoons ground cinnamon
- 1 teaspoon pure vanilla extract
- 1 teaspoon baking powder
- ½ teaspoon baking soda
- ½ teaspoon salt
- ¼ teaspoon ground allspice
- ¼ teaspoon ground nutmeg
- ⅛ teaspoon ground cloves

Directions:

1. Lightly oil a baking tray that will fit in the steamer basket of your Instant Pot.
2. In a bowl, combine the flour, baking powder, baking soda, sugar, cinnamon, allspice, nutmeg, cloves, and salt.
3. In another bowl combine the applesauce, vanilla, and lemon juice.
4. Fold in the diced apples.
5. Stir the wet mixture into the dry mixture slowly until they form a smooth mix.
6. Pour the batter into your baking tray and put the tray in your steamer basket.
7. Pour the minimum amount of water into the base of your Instant Pot and lower the steamer basket.
8. Seal and cook on Steam for 12 minutes.
9. Release the pressure quickly and set to one side to cool a little.

Pina-Colada Cake

Preparation time: 20 Minutes

Servings: 6

Ingredients:

- 2 cups unbleached all-purpose flour
- 1 cup cream of coconut
- 1 cup confectioners' sugar
- ¾ cup canned pineapple, well drained, juice reserved
- ⅓ cup packed light brown sugar or granulated natural sugar
- ¼ cup unsweetened shredded coconut
- 3 tablespoons vegan butter, softened, or vegetable oil
- 1 tablespoon dark rum or 1 teaspoon rum extract
- 1½ teaspoons baking powder
- 1 teaspoon apple cider vinegar
- ½ teaspoon salt
- ½ teaspoon baking soda
- ½ teaspoon coconut extract

Directions:

1. Lightly oil a baking tray that will fit in the steamer basket of your Instant Pot.
2. In a bowl combine the flour, sugar, shredded coconut, baking soda, baking powder, and salt.
3. In another bowl combine the cream of coconut, pineapple juice and flesh, rum, vinegar, and coconut extract.
4. Combine the wet and dry mixes and stir well to ensure they are evenly combined.
5. Pour the batter into your baking tray and put the tray in your steamer basket.
6. Pour the minimum amount of water into the base of your Instant Pot and lower the steamer basket.
7. Seal and cook on Steam for 12 minutes.
8. Release the pressure quickly and set to one side to cool a little.
9. When the cake is cool glaze with a light mix of confectioners' sugar and water.

Pumpkin Spice Cake

Preparation time: 28 Minutes

Servings: 6

Ingredients:

- 1¾ cups unbleached all-purpose flour
- 1 cup canned solid-pack pumpkin
- ¾ cup packed light brown sugar or granulated natural sugar
- ½ cup chopped pecans

- ¼ cup unsweetened almond milk
- ¼ cup vegetable oil
- 1½ teaspoons baking powder
- 1 teaspoon ground cinnamon
- 1 teaspoon pure vanilla extract
- ½ teaspoon salt
- ½ teaspoon ground nutmeg
- ½ teaspoon ground allspice
- ¼ teaspoon ground cloves

Directions:

1. Lightly oil a baking tray that will fit in the steamer basket of your Instant Pot.
2. In a bowl combine the flour, baking powder, cinnamon, nutmeg, allspice, cloves, sugar, and salt.
3. In another bowl combine the pumpkin, oil, almond milk, and vanilla.
4. Mix the wet and dry mixtures together until the mix is evenly smooth.
5. Fold in the pecans.
6. Pour the batter into your baking tray and put the tray in your steamer basket.

7. Pour the minimum amount of water into the base of your Instant Pot and lower the steamer basket.

8. Seal and cook on Steam for 12 minutes.

9. Release the pressure quickly and set to one side to cool a little.

Fudgy Chocolate Cake

Preparation time: 20 Minutes

Servings: 8

Ingredients:

Cake:

- 1½ cups unbleached all-purpose flour
- 1 cup non-dairy milk
- 2/3 cup granulated natural sugar
- ¼ cup unsweetened cocoa powder
- 3 tablespoons vegan butter, softened
- 1½ teaspoons baking powder
- 1 teaspoon pure vanilla extract
- ½ teaspoon cider vinegar
- ¼ teaspoon salt
- ¼ teaspoon baking soda

Frosting:

- ¼ cup unsweetened cocoa powder
- 2 tablespoons vegan butter, melted
- 3 tablespoons non-dairy milk, plus more if needed
- 1 teaspoon pure vanilla extract
- 1½ cups confectioners' sugar, plus more if needed

Directions:

1. Lightly oil a baking tray that will fit in the steamer basket of your Instant Pot.
2. In a bowl combine the flour, cocoa powder, baking soda, baking powder, and salt.
3. Whisk the vegan butter and granulated sugar until they form a creamy blend.
4. Add the milk, vinegar, and vanilla.
5. Add the flour mixture and stir until evenly mixed.
6. Pour the batter into your baking tray and put the tray in your steamer basket.
7. Pour the minimum amount of water into the base of your Instant Pot and lower the steamer basket.
8. Seal and cook on Steam for 12 minutes.

9. Release the pressure quickly and set to one side to cool a little.
10. For the frosting, stir the cocoa into the melted butter until smoothly blended.
11. Add the milk and vanilla and mix well again.
12. Stir in the sugar until you have an almost pourable frosting.
13. Refrigerate until it's time to frost your cake.

Carrot & Pineapple Cake

Preparation time: 20 Minutes

Servings: 6

Ingredients:

- 1½ cups unbleached all-purpose flour
- 2 carrots, peeled and finely shredded (1 cup packed)
- ¾ cup packed light brown sugar or granulated natural sugar
- ½ cup pineapple juice from the chopped pineapple
- ½ cup chopped macadamia nuts
- ⅓ cup canned pineapple, well drained, juice reserved
- ¼ cup vegetable oil

- 1½ teaspoons baking powder
- 1 teaspoon ground cinnamon
- ½ teaspoon salt
- ¼ teaspoon ground nutmeg

Directions:

1. Lightly oil a baking tray that will fit in the steamer basket of your Instant Pot.
2. In a bowl combine the flour, sugar, baking powder, cinnamon, nutmeg, and salt.
3. In another bowl combine the carrot, pineapple, pineapple juice, and oil.
4. Combine the wet and dry mix until a batter forms.
5. Fold in the macadamias.
6. Pour the batter into your baking tray and put the tray in your steamer basket.
7. Pour the minimum amount of water into the base of your Instant Pot and lower the steamer basket.
8. Seal and cook on Steam for 12 minutes.
9. Release the pressure quickly and set to one side to cool a little.

Cream Cheese Frosting

Preparation time: 5 Minutes

Servings: 2.5 cups

Ingredients:

- 1½ cups confectioners' sugar
- 1 cup vegan cream cheese at room temperature
- ½ cup vegan butter, at room temperature
- 1 teaspoon pure vanilla extract

Directions:

1. Combine all the ingredients until smoothly blended.

Orange Polenta Cake

Preparation time: 30 Minutes

Servings: 6

Ingredients:

- 1¼ cups all-purpose flour
- 1 cup unsweetened almond milk
- 2/3 cup plus 1 tablespoon natural sugar
- ⅓ cup fine-ground cornmeal
- ⅓ cup plus 2 tablespoons marmalade
- ¼ cup finely ground almonds
- ¼ cup vegan butter, softened
- 1 navel orange, peeled and sliced into ⅛-inch-thick rounds
- 1½ teaspoons baking powder
- 1 teaspoon pure vanilla extract
- ¾ teaspoon salt

Directions:

1. Lightly oil a baking tray that will fit in the steamer basket of your Instant Pot.
2. Sprinkle a tablespoon of sugar over the base of the baking tray and top with the orange slices.
3. In a bowl combine the flour, cornmeal, baking powder, almonds, and salt.
4. In another bowl combine the remaining sugar, the butter, 1/3 cup of marmalade, and vanilla and mix well. Slowly stir in the almond milk.
5. Combine the wet and dry mixes into a smooth batter.
6. Pour the batter into your baking tray and put the tray in your steamer basket.
7. Pour the minimum amount of water into the base of your Instant Pot and lower the steamer basket.
8. Seal and cook on Steam for 12 minutes.
9. Release the pressure quickly and set to one side to cool a little.
10. Warm the remaining 2 tablespoons of marmalade and brush over the cake.

Peanut Butter & Chocolate Cheesecake

Preparation time: 30 Minutes

Servings: 8

Ingredients:

- 16 ounces vegan cream cheese
- 8 ounces silken tofu, drained
- 1½ cups crushed vegan chocolate cookies
- ¾ cup natural sugar
- ½ cup creamy peanut butter, at room temperature
- ¼ cup unsweetened cocoa powder
- 3 tablespoons vegan butter, melted
- 2 tablespoons hazelnut milk

Directions:

1. Lightly oil a baking tray that will fit in the steamer basket of your Instant Pot.

2. Combine the chocolate crumbs and the butter.

3. Press the chocolate base into your tray.

4. Blend the cream cheese and tofu until smooth.

5. Add the peanut butter, cocoa, hazelnut milk, and sugar to the cheese mix and fold in well.

6. Pour the cheese onto your base and put the tray in your steamer basket.

7. Pour the minimum amount of water into the base of your Instant Pot and lower the steamer basket.

8. Seal and cook on Steam for 15 minutes.

9. Release the pressure quickly and set to one side to cool a little.

Avocado Almond Cabbage Salad

Preparation time: 15 minutes

Cooking time: 0 minutes

Servings: 3

Nutritions:

- Calories 317
- Fat 14.1 g
- Carbohydrates 39.8 g
- Sugar 9.3 g
- Protein 11.6 g
- Cholesterol 0 mg

Ingredients:

- 3 cups savoy cabbage, shredded
- cup ½ blanched almonds
- 1 avocado, chopped
- ¼ tsp pepper
- ¼ tsp sea salt

For Dressings:

- 1 tsp coconut aminos
- ½ tsp Dijon mustard
- 1 tbsp lemon juice
- 3 tbsp olive oil
- Pepper
- Salt

Directions:

1. In a small bowl, mix together all dressing ingredients and set aside.
2. Add all salad ingredients to the large bowl and mix well.
3. Pour dressing over salad and toss well.
4. Serve immediately and enjoy.

Cauliflower Asparagus Soup

Preparation time: 10 minutes

Cooking time: 20 minutes

Servings: 4

Nutritions:

- Calories 74
- Fat 5.6 g
- Carbohydrates 8.9 g
- Sugar 5.1 g
- Protein 3.4 g
- Cholesterol 2 mg

Ingredients:

- 20 asparagus spears, chopped
- 4 cups vegetable stock
- ½ cauliflower head, chopped
- 2 garlic cloves, chopped

- 1 tbsp coconut oil
- Pepper
- Salt

Directions:

1. Heat coconut oil in a large saucepan over medium heat.
2. Add garlic and sauté until softened.
3. Add cauliflower, vegetable stock, pepper, and salt. Stir well and bring to boil.
4. Reduce heat to low and simmer for 20 minutes.
5. Add chopped asparagus and cook until softened.
6. Puree the soup using an immersion blender until smooth and creamy.
7. Stir well and serve warm.

Tomato Asparagus Salad

Preparation time: 5 minutes

Cooking time: 2 minutes

Servings: 4

Nutritions:

- Calories 85
- Fat 7.2 g
- Carbohydrates 5.1 g
- Sugar 2.6 g
- Protein 1.9 g
- Cholesterol 0 mg

Ingredients:

- 1/2 lb asparagus, trimmed and cut into pieces
- 8 oz cherry tomatoes, halved

For Dressings:

- 1/4 tsp garlic and herb seasoning blend
- 1 tbsp vinegar
- 1 tbsp shallot, minced
- 1 garlic clove, minced
- 1 tbsp water
- 2 tbsp olive oil

Directions:

1. Add 1 tablespoon of water and asparagus in a heatproof bowl and cover with cling film and microwave for 2 minutes.
2. Remove asparagus from bowl and place into ice water until cool.
3. Add asparagus and tomatoes into a medium bowl.
4. In a small bowl, mix together all remaining ingredients and pour over vegetables.
5. Toss vegetables well and serve.

Spinach Tomato Stir Fry

Preparation time: 10 minutes

Cooking time: 15 minutes

Servings: 2

Nutritions:

- Calories 104
- Fat 7.1 g
- Carbohydrates 8.9 g
- Sugar 3.6 g
- Protein 4.3 g
- Cholesterol 5 mg

Ingredients:

- 1/2 cup cherry tomatoes, cut in half
- 1/2 onion, sliced
- 4 cups spinach
- 1 garlic clove, diced

- 1/2 tsp lemon zest
- 2 tsp olive oil
- 6 button mushrooms, sliced
- Pepper
- Salt

Directions:

1. Heat olive oil in a pan over medium heat.
2. Add mushrooms and sauté for 3-4 minutes or until lightly browned.
3. Remove mushrooms to a plate and set aside.
4. Add onion and sauté for 2-3 minutes or until softened.
5. Add tomatoes, garlic and lemon zest, and season with pepper and salt. Cook for 2-3 minutes and lightly smashed tomatoes with a spatula.
6. Now add mushrooms and spinach and stir well and cook until spinach is wilted.
7. Season with salt and drizzle with lemon juice.
8. Serve and enjoy.

Celery Salad

Preparation time: 10 minutes

Cooking time: 0 minutes

Servings: 6

Nutritions:

- Calories 38
- Fat 2.5 g
- Carbohydrates 3.3 g
- Sugar 1.5 g
-

- Protein 0.8 g
- Cholesterol 0 mg

Ingredients:

- 6 cups celery, sliced
- ¼ tsp celery seed
- 1 tbsp lemon juice
- 2 tsp lemon zest, grated
- 1 tbsp parsley, chopped
- 1 tbsp olive oil
- Sea salt

Directions:

1. Add all ingredients into the large mixing bowl and toss well.
2. Serve immediately and enjoy.

Brussels sprouts Salad

Preparation time: 20 minutes

Cooking time: 0 minutes

Servings: 6

Nutritions:

- Calories 111
- Fat 7.1 g
- Carbohydrates 11 g
- Sugar 2.7 g
- Protein 4.4 g
- Cholesterol 0 mg

Ingredients:

- 1 ½ lbs Brussels sprouts, trimmed
- ¼ cup toasted hazelnuts, chopped
- 2 tsp Dijon mustard
- 1 ½ tbsp lemon juice

- 2 tbsp olive oil
- Pepper
- Salt

Directions:

1. In a small bowl, whisk together oil, mustard, lemon juice, pepper, and salt.
2. In a large bowl, combine together Brussels sprouts and hazelnuts.
3. Pour dressing over salad and toss well.
4. Serve immediately and enjoy.

www.ingramcontent.com/pod-product-compliance
Lightning Source LLC
Chambersburg PA
CBHW050746030426
42336CB00012B/1678